Religious Topics

FAMILY LIFE

Jon Mayled

Religious Topics

Art and Architecture
Birth Customs
Death Customs
Family Life
Feasting and Fasting
Holy Books

Initiation Rites
Marriage Customs
Pilgrimage
Religious Dress
Religious Services
Teachers and Prophets

First published in 1986 by Wayland (Publishers) Limited
61 Western Road, Hove, East Sussex BN3 1JD, England

© Copyright 1986 Wayland (Publishers) Limited

British Library Cataloguing in Publication Data
Mayled, Jon
   Family life. – (Religious topics)
   1. Family – Religious life – Juvenile
   literature
   I. Title   II. Series
   291.4′4   BV4526.2
   ISBN 0–85078–772–6

Phototypeset by Kalligraphics Ltd., Redhill, Surrey
Printed in Italy by G. Canale & C. S.p.A., Turin
Bound in Belgium by Casterman S.A.

Contents

Introduction   4

Buddhism   6

Christianity   10

Hinduism   14

Islam   18

Judaism   22

Sikhism   27

Glossary   30

Further Reading   31

Index   32

Introduction

For many of us our families are one of the most important parts of our lives. It is our family who look after us, who feed us, and who help us to grow up into adults. For religious people it is often the family who teach them about their religion, and who show them the way of life which is expected of members of that religion.

This Jewish family is celebrating Havdalah, a ceremony held at the end of the Sabbath.

For many people the family is one of the most important parts of their lives.

Our religion affects the way we live and treat other people and also the way in which we worship our God. Our first steps in this religious life take place within the family.

For many religious people, the family is especially important because much of their worship takes place in the home together with their family.

Buddhism

Mahayana and *Theravada* Buddhists live their lives according to the teachings of the Buddha. These teachings are contained in the Three Universal Truths, the Four Noble Truths and the Eightfold Path, which are set out below. They give Buddhists a guide by which to live their lives and achieve peace and understanding.

The Three Universal Truths

Anicca – 'impermanence' – nothing stays the same. Everything in the world is always changing.
Dukka – 'suffering' – there is no way of avoiding pain or disease.
Anatta – 'no soul' – people do not have a soul, just a body.

The Four Noble Truths

Suffering is part of life.
Suffering is caused by being selfish.
Suffering will stop if we stop being selfish.
The way to stop being selfish is to follow the Eightfold Path.

Theravada Buddhists in a temple in Bangkok.

The Eightfold Path

Right Belief	Right Livelihood
Right Resolve	Right Effort
Right Speech	Right Mindfulness
Right Action	Right Concentration

Buddhist families try to live according to these rules. At home people worship each day.

A Buddhist family in their home in Thailand.

They kneel in front of a statue of the Buddha and offer flowers, money or food and light a candle. The worship is usually reading and meditation on a passage from the Buddhist scriptures.

The Buddha taught that prayer itself was useless as there was no-one to whom you could pray.

It is also part of the religious duty of every Buddhist to give food to the *sangha*, the monks. Every day the monks visit the same household to receive food which people willingly give them.

Decorating a roadside shrine.

Young Buddhist monks receiving food in Rangoon, Burma.

Christianity

Above *This picture is of Jesus and his mother Mary.*

Jesus, the founder of Christianity, was born into a fairly poor family who lived in the town of Nazareth in Palestine. As far as we know he spent the first thirty years of his life at home with his parents.

Jesus's parents, Mary and Joseph, are known as the holy family and it is perhaps because of the upbringing which he received that Christians have always considered the family to be a very important part of their religion. Catholics like to have holy statues and pictures in their homes, and often have

A Christian family at home in the Lebanon.

*A nun helps to
prepare a South
American girl for her
First Communion.*

11

Above *The scene on this Christmas card is of a family returning home for Christmas.*

Opposite *Children decorate their Christmas tree in a nursery school in London.*

their house blessed by a priest.

There is no particular act of worship which Christian people celebrate at home with their family, although some families say prayers and read the Bible together. However, many people still say a Grace at the beginning of meals when they eat as a family:

> *Bless us, O Lord, and these Thy gifts which Thou hast given us for our food; through Jesus Christ our Lord. Amen.*

Many Christian communities have a family service on Sunday where all members of the family, adults and children, worship together. Often this may be a form of the Eucharist or Communion Service. This reminds Christians of the Last Supper which Jesus ate with his disciples before he died on the cross.

Christians also celebrate certain festivals connected with important events in Jesus's life, such as Christmas and Easter, in the home with the whole family.

Hinduism

Many Hindus live in what are known as extended families. Several generations of brothers and sisters live together and look after each other. In these families the grandmother is a very important figure, and each evening she may tell the children stories of the Hindu gods.

Women play a very important part in family life as they are entirely responsible for producing the food eaten by the family. The mothers of the family are always shown great respect.

For Hindus, the most important holy place is the home. There may be a room or just a corner set apart for worship. Here there are pictures or statues of the family's favourite gods or goddesses which are decorated with tinsel and lights.

Although women are not allowed to study some of the most holy Hindu scriptures, the

All Hindu homes have a corner set apart for worship.

This Hindu man is worshipping at a shrine in his home in London.

performance of *puja* (worship) is usually their responsibility. In the morning after her bath or shower, she prays and then washes and dresses the statue and offers flowers, incense, light and food to the gods. The food which is given to the gods is called *parshad*. Afterwards, this is added to the rest of the food which the family will eat, so that all the food is blessed. While carrying out these duties the woman may say a prayer called a *mantra*.

These Hindu women are collecting flowers with which to decorate statues of the gods.

In the evening the lamp or *diva* is lit, and many families join together to pray. It is this part of worship which is most important for teaching children about their religion.

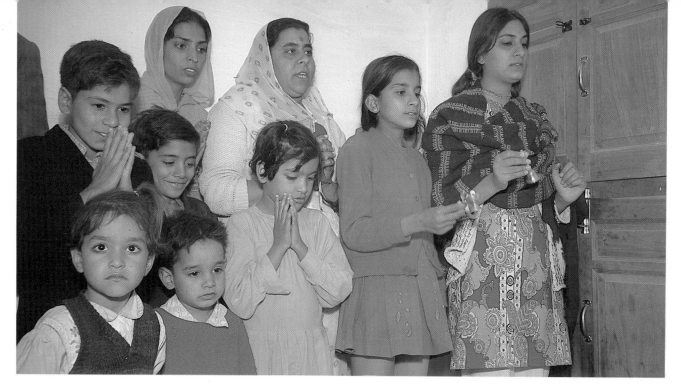

This Hindu family is singing mantras *in the home.*

Sometimes the family may invite a priest to the house to perform a ceremony. The ceremony begins with the priest calling the name of the principal god while a bell is rung and a conch shell blown. Then the gods' feet are washed and they are offered gifts while the people pray.

Women and children may use a rosary of 108 beads – a *mala* – on which they count the names, *Rama*, *Hari* and *Shiva*.

Opposite *A Muslim family outside their home in Bahrain.*

Below *These Muslim boys are reading the* Qur'an, *the Muslim holy book.*

Islam

The family is central to the Islamic religion. Muslims say that when *Allah* (God) created Adam and Eve to live together, he set up the first family unit. Marriage is seen as a very important religious step and most of the prophets of Islam, including Muhammad, were married.

Because the family is so important, women have a special role to play and, according to Muhammad, the people who deserved the best care were:

> *Your mother (he repeated this three times), then your father and then your nearest relatives.*

Each Muslim family has its own copy of the *Qur'an*, the Muslim holy book. This is very important and sacred and is treated with great respect. Copies of the *Qur'an* are often wrapped in a silk cloth to protect them from

ST. MARTIN'S SCHOOL - RESOURCE CENTRE 19

dirt or dust and are placed on a clean, high shelf above all other books. Before reading from the *Qur'an*, Muslims make sure that they are themselves clean.

Special rules on such matters as clothes and food are contained in Islamic law – the *Shar'ia* (the Clear Path). Muslims must eat with the right hand, using the thumb, first and second fingers. The third finger is used when the food is very soft. In the same way people must not blow on hot food to cool it nor say that they do not like a particular food. Children are taught these laws in the same way that children of other religions are

Muslims praying outside a mosque in the USSR.

Muslims say their prayers on a prayer mat. A prayer mat is necessary to ensure that the place of prayer is clean.

taught table manners.

Muslims pray five times a day: *fajr*, at daybreak, *zuhr* at midday, *'asr* in the afternoon, *maghrib* in the evening, and *'isha* at night. Before praying Muslims wash themselves (*wudu*). The prayers are said while facing in the direction of the Kabba in Mecca and are performed in special positions. The daybreak and night prayers will usually take place in the home.

Judaism

Although Jews worship at the synagogue, the centre of their religious life is the home and at the centre of the home is the wife or mother. Jewish children receive most of their religious education at home.

Many Jewish homes have a small box called a *mezuzah* on the right-hand door post of all the doors. This contains a small piece of paper on which is written the *Shema*:

> *Hear, O Israel, the Lord our God, the Lord is One . . .*

People touch the *mezuzah* as they pass it to remind them of God's love.

Jews have strict rules about food and so the kitchen plays an especially important part in Jewish family life. Food which can be eaten is called *kosher* and that which is forbidden by Jewish law is *treife*. No pork or

This Jewish woman is kindling the Sabbath candles whilst her two children look on.

pork products are allowed, and all meat has to be killed in a special way while a prayer is said over it.

In addition, dairy products such as milk, cheese and butter are not eaten at the same meal as meat. In the kitchen of a Jewish home you will find two sets of kitchen equipment, one for meat and the other for dairy foods.

One of the most important aspects of Jewish life is the Sabbath meal, *Shabbat*, which takes place every week. The Sabbath

The Havdalah *service is held at the end of the Sabbath.*

takes place from dusk on Friday to dusk on Saturday, and there are very strict rules about what can be done on that day. People may not cook, sew, light a fire, start a car, carry things outside or write. This makes sure that they have plenty of time to rest and to think about God.

On Friday the house is cleaned, clothes are washed and food is cooked so that everything is ready. A clean, white table-cloth is placed on the table and two candles are put there along with wine, two challot loaves covered by a cloth, and salt as the bread is later dipped in salt. A few minutes before sunset, which is the beginning of the Sabbath, the mother of the family lights the candles. When the sun has gone down she says the blessing.

Blessed are you, Lord our God, King of the Universe, who has blessed us with His Commandments and has commanded us to light the Sabbath candles.

The family then attend a short service at

A Jewish couple with their baby in Masada, Israel.

25

the synagogue. After this they return home for the evening meal. This is a large and special feast which begins with wine and bread being blessed. The Sabbath ends with the *Havdalah* service.

Another very important festival in the home is *Pesach* or Passover. For nine days Jews remember their escape from slavery in Egypt as told in the book of Exodus. Because the Israelites left in such a hurry there was no time for the bread dough to rise and so, before the feast of *Pesach*, Jews ensure that there is no *chametz*, food or grains which can be leavened, or made to rise, in the house.

This Jewish father is blessing the wine before the feast of Pesach.

Sikhism

Sikh family life is an important part of their religion and culture. It is the duty of a Sikh husband to provide his wife with a home and the parents will continue to expect regular visits from their children.

Girls are often expected to spend most of their time at home in the evenings. Their mothers teach them how to become good wives; how to cook, sew and embroider. A Sikh mother sees this teaching as her responsibility and not that of a school.

A Sikh family at their home in Birmingham. It is the duty of every Sikh husband to provide his wife and family with a home.

A Sikh bride prepares for her wedding. Weddings are a family occasion for all religions.

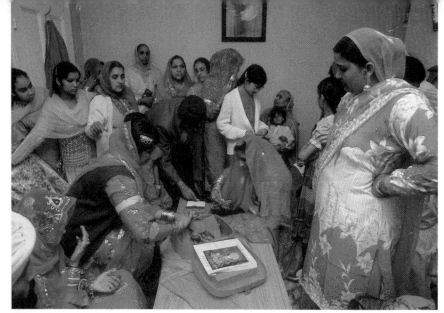

Below *A drawing of Guru Nanak, the founder of Sikhism.*

Sikhs will pray at least twice each day. In the morning, after washing, they repeat the two prayers, the *japji* and the *jap*. Next they meditate on the founder of Sikhism, *Guru Nanak*, and repeat a poem called the *asa-di-var*.

In the evenings they say the hymn called the *Rahiras* and before going to bed, the *Sohilla*. Some Sikhs also use a *mala*, a loop of cotton with 108 knots in it. As they come to each knot Sikhs say:

'Wahe Guru' – Wonderful Lord

A reading of the Guru Granth Sahib *in the Golden Temple of Amritsar in India.*

If the family has a copy of the *Guru Granth Sahib*, the Sikh holy book, they may sit around it for readings and prayers in the evening.

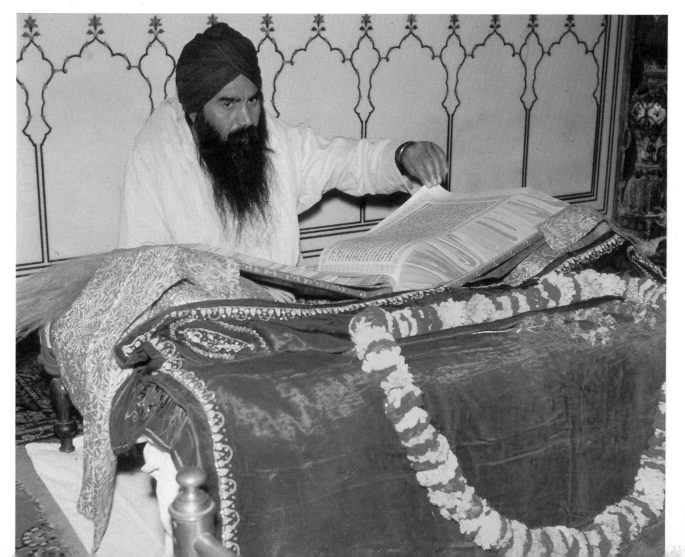

Glossary

Allah The Muslim name for God.

Asa-di-var A Sikh religious poem.

Buddha Siddartha Gautama – the founder of Buddhism.

Communion A Christian service which remembers the Last Supper Jesus ate with his disciples before he died.

Grace A prayer of thanksgiving said by Christians before a meal.

Guru Granth Sahib The Sikh holy book.

Havdalah A Jewish ceremony which marks the end of the Sabbath.

Jesus The founder of Christianity.

Kosher Food which has been prepared according to Jewish law.

Mala A string of beads or knots used in prayers.

Mecca The Muslim holy city in Saudi Arabia.

Muhammad The founder of Islam.

Passover A Jewish festival which celebrates the escape from Egypt.

Puja The main Hindu form of worship which often takes place in the home. Prayers are offered and flowers and food are placed before a statue of a god.

Qur'an The Muslim holy book.

Sangha Buddhist monks.

Shabbat The Jewish day of rest.

Shar'ia The Islamic law.

Shema The most important Jewish prayer. It is the first learned by children and the last spoken by the dying.

Treife Food which Jews are not allowed to eat.

Wudu The washing before Muslim prayer.

Acknowledgements

The Publisher would like to thank the following for providing the pictures for the book: The Hutchison Library 9 (both), 11, 13, 14, 15, 18, 21, 25, 28 (right); Preben Kristensen 8, 19; Christine Osborne 10 (right; Anne and Bury Peerless 17, 27, 28 (left); Picturebank Library 5; Topham 12; Zefa 4, 7, 10 (left), 16, 20, 23, 24, 26, 29.

Further Reading

If you would like to find out more about family life, you may like to read the following books:

Beliefs and Believers series – Wayland

Exploring Religion series – Bell and Hyman

Religions of the World series – Wayland

Worship series – Holt Saunders

Man and Religion series – part one – RMEP

The following videos are very helpful:

Islam – produced by ILEA Learning Resources

The Jesus Project – produced by CEM Video, 2 Chester House, Pages Lane, London N10

Through the Eyes – produced by CEM video

Index

Buddhism
  Buddha, The 6, 9, 30
  Eightfold Path 6, 8
  family worship 8–9
  Four Noble Truths 6, 7
  Mahayana Buddhists 6
  sangha (monks) 9, 30
  Theravada Buddhists 6
  Three Universal Truths 6

Christianity
  Bible, The 12
  Christmas 12, 13
  Communion 12, 30
  Easter 12
  family worship 10, 12
  Grace 12, 30
  Jesus 10, 12, 30
  Roman Catholics 10

Hinduism
  diva 16
  extended families 14
  family life 14–17
  gods 14, 15, 17
  mantra 15
  parshad 15
  puja 15, 30

Islam
  Allah (God) 18, 30
  Kabba 21
  Mecca 21, 30
  Muhammad 18, 30
  prayers
    'asr 21
    fajr 21
    'isha 21
    maghrib 21
    zuhr 21
  Qur'an 18, 20, 30
  Shar'ia 20, 30
  women 18
  wudu 21, 31

Judaism
  family life 22, 25–6
  food
    chametz 26
    kosher 22, 30
    treife 22, 31
  Havdalah 26, 30
  mezuzah 22
  Pesach 26
  Sabbath 24–5
  Shema 22, 30
  synagogue 22, 26

Sikhism
  asa-di-var 28, 30
  family life 27
  Guru Nanak 28
  Guru Granth Sahib 29, 30
  mala 28, 30
  prayers
    jap 28
    japji 28
    Rahiras 28
    Sohilla 28